THE
5-Minute Happiness Journal

Practices to Help You Tap Into Joy Every Day

LESLIE MARCHAND, LCSW

ROCKRIDGE PRESS

For general information on our other products and services or to obtain technical support, please contact our Customer Care Department within the United States at (866) 744-2665, or outside the United States at (510) 253-0500.

Interior and Cover Designer: Antonio Valverde
Art Producer: Janice Ackerman
Editor: Emily Angell
Production Editor: Emily Sheehan

All images used under license © Shutterstock and © iStock.
Author Photo: © 2019 Amanda Faucett.

ISBN: Print 978-1-64611-749-9

R0

This Journal Belongs to:

_____

Contents

So many conditions of happiness are available—more than enough for you to be happy right now. You don't have to run into the future in order to get more.

———

Thich Nhat Hanh

Introduction

Welcome to *The 5-Minute Happiness Journal*. The fact that you are reading this tells me that you're committed to bringing more happiness and joy into your life—good for you! I believe that each of us has a right to find and live in our own happiness. Journaling provides a wonderful vehicle through which we can reflect and explore what happiness means to us, where to find it, and how we can harness it in our lives.

Through the centuries, philosophers and psychologists have espoused the ideals of happiness and joy as life-giving forces and debated the causes and effects in great depth. In our modern society, the definition of happiness has become skewed. It's too easy to think that happiness is either the ability to feel good all of the time or the absence of challenges in life—neither of which is a realistic scenario.

Understanding and experiencing happiness is nuanced, varying from person to person and depending on our personalities, life experiences, and interests. As members of a society so drastically influenced by outside forces—cultural norms, unrealistic "celebrity" ideals, consumerism, and social media, to name a few—we can all benefit from revisiting the true definition of happiness and pause to consider how we can personally experience it in a unique way. Positive psychology researcher Sonja Lyubomirsky defines happiness as "*the experience of joy, contentment, or positive well-being, combined with a sense that one's life is good, meaningful, and worthwhile.*"

Happiness is the experience of joy and meaning in the midst of the messy middle of life. It encompasses both the feeling and experience of happiness in the moment, as well as an enduring sense of happiness and fulfillment as a person. To take it a step further, it's the ability to see the good in things, even the most difficult of life circumstances. Happiness is the ability to find peace with the past, contentment in the present, and hope for the future. It's a deep sense of satisfaction in who you are as a person, how you relate to family and friends, and the value that you give and receive in the work and activities of your daily life.

So how do you find joy in the everyday, no matter what? You make a choice. You practice. You learn new skills and tools. You keep moving forward, living life one day at a time. And in it all, you look for the good—the light, the helpers, the rainbow, the smile on someone's face. You allow yourself to feel your feelings—the good ones and the not-so-good ones. You learn how to deal with life's challenges, move through them, and remain happy in the midst of them. It may sound far-fetched or even unattainable but there is a science behind joy and happiness that shows how you can get there.

I have always been interested in human behavior and personal growth, both for my own sense of well-being and to better serve people through my work as a licensed clinical social worker. The training to become a therapist tends to focus on people's problems and challenges and how these challenges impact a person as well as on the skills and interventions to help them overcome those same challenges. But exciting things are happening in the field. The emerging field of positive psychology focuses not only on how to help people overcome their challenges but on how to help them live lives of happiness, joy, and fulfillment. The field of neuroscience is developing at a rapid pace and is teaching us that we can rewire the neural pathways in our brains through intentional practices. The research in these fields gives me, and many other practitioners, hope that every person possesses the ability to step into this life of happiness and joy.

I started studying happiness, positive psychology, and neuroscience at a much deeper level several years ago after going through some difficult life transitions of my own. By integrating some of the tenets and philosophies of these fields in my own life, I found that I settled into a rhythm with my family, career, and pursuit of my own dreams, goals, and, of course, happiness. I took the time and energy to ask the questions "what makes me happy?" and "how can I help other people find a deeper sense of happiness?" I took the Science of Happiness course the first time that it was offered by the Greater Good Science Center. I read every book I could find on the different aspects of happiness and a meaningful life. I applied the principles to myself and started teaching them to my kids, friends, clients, and students. I also became more intentional in my mindset and the way I spent my time on a daily basis. My life has always been very full. As you can probably relate, I don't always have time for a full hour of daily practices or the ability to take a vacation or go for a spa day. Instead, I've made a commitment to practices that take only a few minutes at a time, and I'm excited to share some of my favorites with you.

In this journal, I'll share prompts and practices that you can do in five minutes once a day, or several times throughout the day, to boost your happiness. These prompts and practices are divided into four sections: reflecting on personal happiness from within, embracing the joy in your life, finding the happiness in the world around you, and practicing gratitude in the everyday.

Although they can be immensely helpful, the prompts and practices in this journal are not intended as a substitute for therapy or medical treatment. Please get professional help if you have a deep sense of sadness or anxiety or another mental health condition. We all need support, so don't hesitate to get the help that you need from a qualified medical professional and/or licensed therapist.

Whether you are going through a hard time right now or you are simply looking for ways to experience more happiness, I am grateful for your presence and hope that this journal guides you on an introspective journey toward a deeper sense of joy, meaning, and gratitude in your life.

Happiness Is an Inside Job

appiness is a state of mind. It's a way of being and a very personal experience. What makes you happy may be very different from what makes me happy. You have the right to define happiness for yourself, and you have the freedom and responsibility to find and create happiness in your own life on a daily basis. Don't worry if this sounds like a tall order. We're going to walk through the process together.

The journal prompts in this section will help you discover what really brings you joy and contentment. We'll look at how you can make powerful shifts in your perspective and take action to feel a sense of positive well-being. You'll explore what's important to you when it comes to living a life of purpose and meaning. As you discover what makes you happy, you'll gain clarity on the steps you can take to experience happiness more fully, authentically, and consistently.

Happiness depends upon ourselves.

—

Aristotle

What makes you happy? Start listing your stream-of-consciousness thoughts—that is, write them all as they come, and don't filter anything out. Notice what makes you smile as you write, even if it seems out-landish or unrealistic. See if you can write for 5 minutes without stopping.

We all have areas of our lives in which we are happy and other areas that may be more challenging or burdensome. Generally speaking, however, are you happy with your life right now? If there are specific aspects of your life where you really feel happy, write about them here.

_____

_____

_____

_____

_____

_____

_____

_____

_____

_____

_____

_____

_____

_____

Are there certain aspects of life that are challenging right now? What are they, and how do these aspects of life create a barrier to your happiness?

If you had a magic wand, what areas of your life would need to shift and align so you would be happy at this time?

_____

_____

_____

_____

_____

_____

_____

_____

_____

_____

_____

_____

_____

_____

_____

_____

_____

What are your goals around happiness? What will your life look and feel like when you experience happiness more fully and consistently?

List 3 activities that you do or would like to do on a regular basis that give you a sense of purpose and meaning. These can be focused on your health, relationships, work, volunteer activities, or hobbies of any sort.

"State of Happiness" Mindfulness Practice

Sit in a comfortable seated position. Close your eyes and relax your body. Take 3 deep breaths. Feel your shoulders relax. Notice that it's possible to experience happiness in this moment. Simply be present in the moment and feel the sensations in your body. Allow the corners of your mouth to turn upward. Feel a sense of warmth and joy in your heart. Notice the thoughts moving through your mind without judging them. Any thought, feeling, or sensation is okay. Take 3 more deep breaths and gently open your eyes.

Happiness is a state of mind, a choice, a way of living; it is not something to be achieved, it is something to be experienced.

—

Steve Maraboli

If happiness is a choice, do you ever feel any resistance to choosing happiness? Do you have times where you focus on a problem or situation that brings about sadness or unhappiness? Be honest and gentle with yourself.

Our happiness depends heavily on our perspective; how we view or perceive a situation. Any situation in our lives can be considered pleasant, unpleasant, or neutral.

Write a sentence or two that describes a situation in your life that has a neutral emotional impact.

_____

_____

_____

_____

_____

_____

Now think about the situation again as if it was unpleasant. Imagine that a slight shift in how the situation played out left you with a bad taste in your mouth. How do you feel? What sensations do you notice in your body?

Clear your mind. Imagine the situation a third time as if it was a pleasant experience. What slight shift would allow you to walk away with a smile on your face. How do you feel? What sensations do you notice in your body? Notice how your thoughts can affect your feelings and bodily sensations.

See The Big Picture

Take 5 minutes to imagine that you can watch yourself
as you go about your normal activities for an entire day.
Watch yourself wake up, get ready, interact with family
and friends, and do the activities that are meaningful
for you. Notice how many lives you touch. Pay attention
to the impact that your actions have on other people.
Reflect on how you feel at the end of this exercise.

The Colors in
Your Kaleidoscope

Following is a drawing of a kaleidoscope. In each petal, write one element of your life—this may include family, friends, work, hobbies, home, pets, etc. Color in the different fragments depending on how happy they make you in this moment. The happier the petal, the brighter the color. While some areas of your life may be happier than others, notice how parts of your life look when put in perspective of the whole of your life.

We cannot be happy if we expect to live all the time at the highest peak of intensity. Happiness is not a matter of intensity but of balance and order and rhythm and harmony.

———

Thomas Merton

Write down 3 to 5 things in your everyday life that bring you happiness. Consider the little things, like waking up and enjoying a cup of coffee in silence before you start your day, or noticing the beauty of the leaves on a tree as you drive to work. Keep adding to this list as new "happiness triggers" come up for you.

Simple can be harder than complex: You have to work hard to get your thinking clean to make it simple. But it's worth it in the end because once you get there, you can move mountains.

—

Steve Jobs

Sometimes we think of happiness as a complicated mission, something that we have to work hard to achieve. Let's keep it simple. In 1 or 2 sentences, write down what makes you happy about where you are at this very moment in your life.

Contrast is an important concept when it comes to understanding happiness. Our brains can understand one thing more deeply when it's in contrast to its opposite or something very different. Write about an experience in your life in which you became acutely aware of your own happiness in contrast with another time in your life. For example, you might be happy to be home after traveling for an extended period of time or grateful to feel healthy after recovering from a cold.

Write about a time in your life when a closed door led to a new opportunity that brought more happiness in your life.

When one door of happiness closes, another opens; but often we look so long at the closed door that we do not see the one which has been opened for us.

Helen Keller

Are there situations in which you feel unhappy on a consistent basis? An example might be a feeling of unhappiness every Monday morning as you end your weekend and return to work. It's possible to shift your feelings by taking action. You might change the feeling of unhappiness by playing your favorite song as you drive into work. Write about a situation that causes you some unhappiness in your day-to-day life and a way that you can take a specific action to shift your feelings toward happiness.

What is one easy activity that brings you happiness? This activity should be something that you can do anytime in 5 minutes or less, in any place, and without any special equipment. What about this activity brings you happiness?

Take 5 minutes to do the activity that you wrote about in the previous prompt. Was there an immediate lift in your mood? Notice how you feel afterward, and jot those feelings down.

Happiness is
determined more
by one's state
of mind than
external events.

—

Dalai Lama XIV

When we talk about happiness as an "inside job," that means that you, and you alone, are the person responsible for your happiness. It's easy to rely on someone else for our happiness or to blame someone else when we aren't happy. Have you ever done this? Write about your experience.

You might get some pushback from people in your life when you decide to focus on your own happiness. Has this ever happened to you? How can you respond to people who judge the things you do for the sake of your own happiness?

Many of us believe that we have to be doing something productive ALL of the time. You might even feel guilty for taking time to do something for the sheer pleasure of the activity. Do you ever feel this way? Take a few minutes to jot down your thoughts.

The past several prompts have brought to light ways in which you might hold back from allowing yourself to experience happiness. Now it's time to make a change. Write a letter to yourself that gives you permission to focus on your own happiness, meaningful activities, and pleasure.

Dear _____

YOUR NAME HERE

_____

_____

_____

_____

_____

_____

Love,

_____

YOUR NAME HERE

Move for Your Mood

A new research study suggests that "feeling active" is an important factor in well-being and even longevity. Think about one activity that energizes you and improves your mood. A quick walk around the block? A restorative yoga pose? Some simple stretches? Take 5 to 10 minutes to do that activity now. Think about how it made you feel. What specifically did it do to energize you? How did it improve your mood?

The definition of happiness includes the "experience of joy" and a "sense that one's life is meaningful." This means that true happiness involves **both** the momentary experience and a larger sense of purpose. Write down at least two activities that take 5 minutes or less: one that gives you an experience of joy and another that gives you a sense of purpose and meaning.

Pick one of the activities in this section, and commit to spending 5 to 10 minutes doing that activity at a specific time and place each day for the next week. Using the lines below, write down your commitment in this format: "I will _____ (activity) at _____ (time) in _____ (location) every day for the next week." Make a few notes below about how you feel each day after doing that activity.

Write your own mantra, or motto, about seeing happiness as an inside job. This is 1 or 2 sentences that remind you that it's okay to focus on your own happiness. It can be as simple as "I am responsible for my happiness" or "I will do what I love and find my own joy in each experience today."

Embrace Where You Are

hen we embrace happiness, we take it in and include it as a part of our whole life. To embrace is to do much more than just tolerate. To embrace is to lean in, to take a leap, to say yes, and to look for and expect the good.

We all know that life has its share of ups and downs, good and bad, light and dark. Nobody is immune to these highs and lows, but I believe that we can make a choice each and every day. Happiness is found in choosing to be fully present and embracing of this moment—right here, right now.

In order to experience happiness, we have to be willing and able to feel all of our emotions. It requires skill and sometimes courage to feel your feelings, to deal with them directly, and to heal any negative emotions so that you can return to a state of happiness. This section will help you to embrace all of life.

Happiness is a state of mind. It's just according to the way you look at things.

—

Walt Disney

Seek and Embrace

When you embrace life, you often receive an embrace in return. Take at least 5 minutes today to practice embracing and notice the giving and receiving that is involved. This could be an actual embrace, such as a hug with a loved one, a conversation with a close friend, or even a quick dip in a hot bath that lets the water soften and relax your muscles.

Write a few sentences about your perspective on embracing ALL of life. Does it come easily to you? Are there areas where you feel a sense of resistance?

Inspire Yourself

Think about what inspires you. Is it reading a passage from an autobiography of an important historical figure? Listening to an upbeat song? Learning a new skill that engages your mind and creativity? Pick an activity that inspires you and take at least a few minutes to practice it today.

And when you sense a faint potentiality for happiness after such dark times you must grab onto the ankles of that happiness and not let go until it drags you face-first out of the dirt— this is not selfishness, but obligation. You were given life; it is your duty to find something beautiful within life no matter how slight.

———

Elizabeth Gilbert

Describe a time in your life when you went through something difficult but were eventually able to embrace the experience, feel gratitude for the lessons, and see the beauty in it. How did you participate in creating your own happiness?

Write about a long-term goal that will make you happy. Describe how the journey toward the goal will bring you happiness even before you accomplish your goal.

_____

_____

_____

_____

_____

_____

_____

_____

_____

_____

_____

_____

Life-Affirming Mantra

Come up with a short mantra or motto about how you are going to embrace your journey moving forward. An example might be: "Every day has good and bad, but I am lucky to be living life. I will embrace it all and find the bright side in every challenge." Spend 5 minutes thinking about your personal mantra in silence as you slowly breathe in and out. Write it on an index card or sticky note and put it somewhere you can see it on a daily basis.

There's a part of our brain and nervous system called the reticular activating system. It helps the mind filter out thoughts, ideas, and memories that aren't important and keep ones that are important. If you are focused on looking for happiness, your mind will find more happiness.

Write a few sentences about how you picture happiness in your life. Is it being surrounded by family and friends? Having a productive day at work? Showing up for your weekly yoga class? Try to be conscious of what makes you happy, and then notice throughout the day when you find more of that type of happiness in your life.

Think about a situation in your life that has been challenging. Is there something good that came into your life as a result? Write about how the situation may have ultimately helped you in some way. Set an intention to remember the positive lessons of the challenging situation every time you think about that experience.

Memory Lane Meditation

Sit in a comfortable and relaxed position. You can even lie down for this practice. Allow your mind to wander back to your childhood. Find a memory that makes you smile and possibly laugh. Play out the scene again in your mind. Allow yourself to feel the happy feelings that you felt at that time.

In order to feel anything, we have to have the capacity to feel everything. When you numb one emotion that you don't want to feel, it tends to numb even the emotions that you do want to feel—such as happiness. Are you able to allow yourself to feel sadness and other more complex emotions? Write about whatever comes up for you.

A Mindfulness Practice
to Embrace Life

Sit in a comfortable position. Lengthen your spine and relax your shoulders. Close your eyes and bring your awareness to your breath. As you breathe in, imagine the breath filling your lungs and every cell of your body as you take in all that life has to offer. As you breathe out, imagine letting go of judgment and fear. Squeeze your belly back toward your spine as you exhale and release. Inhale again; exhale. Repeat this process several times. When you feel ready, let your body fully relax, and allow your breath to return to its normal pace. Bring your concentration back to this moment. Open your eyes and notice how you feel.

Have you ever had an epiphany—a time when you suddenly understood the essential nature or meaning of something in your life? Write about a time when you gained clarity in the midst of, or after, a time of confusion, uncertainty, or challenge.

Elise Ballard, author of *Epiphany*, has a formula for creating an epiphany experience:

Your belief in possibility + action = manifestation

What do you believe is possible when it comes to having more happiness in your life? Write it down. What's one action step you can take toward creating that type of happiness? Write that down. Take 5 minutes every day for the next week to take that action step. Notice how happy you feel, and write about it.

Feel It, Deal with It, Heal It

The next three journal prompts will walk you through a process that I developed to help you shift your emotional response to difficult circumstances. In order to fully embrace where you are, you need to be willing and able to feel your feelings, positively deal with those feelings, and take steps to heal any negative feelings associated with certain life experiences.

First, think of a recent experience that prompted strong negative emotions. Go back and feel those feelings. Write about the situation that prompted them.

List the feelings that you felt at the time of the experience you wrote about in the previous prompt. As an example, you may have felt sadness, frustration, anger, or fear. Take a moment to actually feel those feelings again. Now think about an action step that you can take to help you deal with the feelings. For example, if you were feeling frustration or anger, perhaps you could write those feelings on a piece of paper and tear it up. If you were feeling sad, you could tell a close friend about the experience and allow the friend to support you.

Finally, how can you heal those feelings and shift them toward happiness? This may just be a matter of noticing the feelings and releasing them. Or, perhaps you can shift your perspective and see something positive that resulted from the experience that you hadn't noticed before. Maybe you are simply grateful that you are no longer experiencing that event, and you know that it helped you become more resilient. Whatever it is for you, reflect on and write about it.

To be nobody-but-yourself—in a world which is doing its best, night and day, to make you everybody else—means to fight the hardest battle which any human being can fight. . .

—

E.E. Cummings

Write down one thing you do regularly that makes you happy, even if other people think you should be doing something else with your time.

There may be things that are holding you back from stepping into your own happiness and joy. Write down the first thing that comes to mind. Reflect on it. Write more about it if you wish.

Is there a benefit you receive from not fully stepping into your own happiness or joy? Is there fear? Are you unfamiliar with what it feels like to be happy? Do you have friends or family who focus more on being unhappy? Will you be judged for being too happy-go-lucky?

Reflecting on the previous prompt, what would it feel like if you let go of this fear or reason for holding back? How would your life change? Would you be happier?

_____

_____

_____

_____

_____

_____

_____

_____

_____

_____

_____

_____

_____

_____

Imagination is a powerful gift. It allows you to tap into your creative ability to form an idea that doesn't exist yet in reality. Write about a time when you used your imagination to solve a problem or do something in a way that you had never thought to do it before.

Use your imagination to create a mental image of what happiness looks and feels like for you. Write about your image.

_____

_____

_____

_____

_____

_____

_____

_____

_____

_____

_____

_____

_____

_____

Sense Happiness

Now that you have a mental image of what happiness looks like for you, expand this image and experience it with all 5 of your senses. Close your eyes if it helps you to be more present during this practice. What do you see when you are happy? What do you hear, taste, and smell? What do you feel, both in a tactile sense of feeling your surroundings and in a physical sense of feeling the happiness in your emotions and bodily sensations.

Joyful Artistry

Take out a piece of paper and some colored pens or pencils, or choose any visual art medium—even digital design will work. You may also use the box on the opposite page. Draw a picture of what happiness looks like to you. Let go of perfection and judgment. Let this be fun and freeing as you allow your creativity to flow.

As human beings, our job in life is to help people realize how rare and valuable each one of us really is, that each of us has something that no one else has—or ever will have—something inside that is unique to all time. It's our job to encourage each other to discover that uniqueness and to provide ways of developing its expression.

———

Fred Rogers (Mr. Rogers)

What is something unique about you that makes you happy? Describe how and why it makes you happy.

Think of a friend or a family member and what makes them unique. Describe how their unique traits make you happy. Share your words with that person. Encourage each other to embrace your own uniqueness.

Write a short mantra about what makes you unique and happy. Start with the phrase "I am. . ." and make a bold statement of who you are as someone who pursues happiness and joy on a daily basis.

Connect with the World around You

While I believe Aristotle's statement that happiness depends on ourselves, I also know that connecting with the world around us is important. There's an important distinction between relying on other people for happiness and reaching out to connect with people we love—people who have common interests and who help us have a positive perspective on life.

In order to truly connect to other people and the world around you, it is essential to first know who you are and what makes you happy. Through the exercises in the first two sections of this journal, you have discovered more about what makes you uniquely happy. Now we will turn our focus to different aspects of life that create a sense of belonging, connection, and happiness. We will focus on family, friends, work, hobbies, community service, nature, and using all of your senses to fully participate in life's experiences.

Ye live not for yourselves; a thousand fibres connect you with your fellow-men, and along those fibers, as along sympathetic threads, run your actions as causes, and return to you as effects.

—

Henry Melville

Write a few sentences about how you contribute to your family's happiness and how your family contributes to your happiness. Note that this doesn't need to be limited to family in the traditional sense of the word. It can be your partner, your roommate, or your innermost circle.

List three traits that you look for in a friend. If these are the most important traits that you look for in others, then you likely possess those traits as well. Write about how you exhibit those traits in your friendships and in your life.

_____

_____

_____

_____

_____

_____

_____

_____

_____

_____

_____

Make One Small Change

Look around the room in your home where you spend the most time. What's one small change that you can make that will bring you a sense of happiness—buying a plant, cutting flowers from your garden, lighting a candle, straightening up the papers on your desk, clearing off surfaces, or hanging a picture? Take a few minutes to make a small change now.

List 3 friends who contribute to your happiness. Write one memory of happy times with each of them.

Do you have a close friend with whom you feel content and at peace when you are together, no matter what you are doing? Write a few sentences about what makes your friendship so special.

Laughter Boost

Making yourself voluntarily laugh may have the same physiological and psychological benefits as laughing at a funny joke. Yes, it may feel silly, but you're going to have to trust me on this one. Test it out and see what you notice about your level of happiness. Laugh out loud. Listen to the sound of your voice. Feel the vibration in your body. Get a friend or family member to join you, and notice how you feel.

Think about someone in your life who inspires you. If you could adopt one of their personality traits, what would it be? How would this trait improve your level of happiness?

"I Am Loved"
Affirmation

Write the following affirmation down on a sticky note or index card so you can see it and repeat it often. Feel free to adjust the wording to fit your life: "My family and friends love me, and I love myself. I experience happiness and share it with others." Sit with this thought for 5 minutes. Slowly breathe in and out. If your mind wanders, gently bring it back to the affirmation.

Think back to the time when you made the decision to pursue your current career or role that fills the majority of your time. What were you looking forward to at the time in relation to your own happiness and fulfillment?

Do you still experience the same sense of happiness and fulfillment in your work or current role as you did when you began? If not, is there a shift you can make that will bring you more happiness?

_____

_____

_____

_____

_____

_____

_____

_____

_____

_____

What circumstances related to your work or role contribute to your happiness? For example, you could have a positive relationship with your colleagues, a flexible schedule to accommodate your family responsibilities, or an income that allows you to pay your bills and have money for entertainment.

Action may not
always bring
happiness,
but there is
no happiness
without action.

———

William James

We all know that work settings are not perfect, as there are many factors outside of our control. Despite this fact, you can still take actions that improve your happiness. Write down one 5-minute action that you can do today that will bring you more happiness in your work setting or setting where you spend the majority of your time.

Connect with a Colleague

Take 5 minutes and connect with a colleague or friend who is in a similar role as you. Share what you enjoy most about your current role, and ask them to share the same with you.

What is your favorite hobby? What about it makes you happy? How often do you participate in this activity?

What is a hobby that you've always wanted to try but haven't yet? Write down the hobby. Why does it interest you?

_____

_____

_____

_____

_____

_____

_____

_____

_____

_____

_____

Do the Duchenne

Have you ever noticed that a truly happy person smiles with their mouth *and* their eyes? Scientists have a name for the type of smile that uses the muscles around both the mouth and eyes. It's called the Duchenne smile, and it signals true enjoyment. Practice smiling with your mouth and your eyes. I find the easiest way to do this is to find a short video of a baby laughing. I find myself instantly smiling and notice an immediate shift in my mood.

Which of your five senses do you notice the most—sight, sound, taste, touch, or smell? Write down the first thing that comes to you. For example, some people are very visual and enjoy the visual arts, and others are interested in music and everything related to sound, while others appreciate taste and everything related to the culinary arts.

Experiences, Not Things

Research tells us that we derive more happiness from experiences than we do from belongings. Take 5 minutes to participate in an activity that uses the sense that you connect with the most. You might light a candle if you love its smell, listen to a song that brings you joy, or slowly savor a small portion of your favorite comfort food.

Happiness lies not in the mere possession of money; it lies in the joy of achievement, in the thrill of creative effort.

—

Franklin D. Roosevelt

Whether through work or hobbies, many people feel a sense of happiness when they accomplish or create something. Write about a recent accomplishment that gave you a sense of pride and joy.

People often say that it is better to give than to receive. I believe that we all need a balance of giving and receiving. Reflect on a time recently when you gave to someone and made them incredibly happy, and when you received a gift or gesture that made your heart swell.

_____

_____

_____

_____

_____

_____

_____

_____

_____

_____

_____

_____

_____

_____

Reconnect with the World around You

Sit outside or in a place where you have a view of the outdoors. Notice the sun that rises and sets every day, and how it provides light and warmth and the ability to distinguish day from night. Notice the ground and all that grows in order to provide food, oxygen, and shelter for all living things. Notice the buildings and structures that people and animals create to give us space to live, work, eat, and commune with one another. Breathe it in with all your senses as you notice your part in nature, community, and all that is around you.

What is one way that you consistenly give to the people closest to you? Do you feel happy when you are giving to your friends and family? How does it make you feel? Conversely, how do these people give to you? How does that make you feel?

_____

_____

_____

_____

_____

_____

_____

_____

_____

_____

_____

_____

_____

_____

Pay It Forward

Take 5 minutes to show kindness to another person. It can be as simple as making eye contact and smiling at a stranger, making your colleague a cup of tea, or checking on a neighbor who is under the weather. Notice how you feel.

I have found that among its other benefits, giving liberates the soul of the giver.

——

Maya Angelou

What is a form of community service or philanthropy that you enjoy? How does giving in this way contribute to your happiness?

"You are not just a drop in the ocean, you are the mighty ocean in the drop." —Rumi

Think about this quote as an affirmation of your connection to the world around you. You are a drop, an individual, a whole person in and of yourself. You are the ocean, a powerful force that connects every living thing across every continent on earth. You are connected to all of life, and you contribute to its ebb and flow every day. What other thoughts about connection does this quote bring up for you?

Be Grateful:
Find Joy Every Day

Gratitude has the power to change our lives. It's that simple. Practicing gratitude every day can improve our physical health, increase our mental strength, help us cope with stress, help us sleep better, enhance our empathy, and regulate our emotions.

We can intentionally practice and culti-vate gratitude and reap the benefits in every area of our lives. Research even suggests that the benefits of gratitude grow over time and have a lasting effect on the brain. If you are looking to create just one new habit that leads to greater happiness, physical health, emotional health, and an overall sense of well-being, look no further than gratitude. In this section, you will learn practices for building gratitude into your life and, with that, experience more happiness and joy on a daily basis.

Gratitude is a
powerful catalyst
for happiness.
It's the spark that
lights a fire of joy in
your soul.

——

Amy Collette

Belief in your ability to create and maintain a new habit is an important part of the formula for creating or changing habits. Do you believe that establishing a gratitude practice can change your life? List a few benefits of gratitude that you would like to enjoy in your life.

Showing appreciation for other people can help deepen our relationships. Think about an acquaintance or someone you met recently and see on a regular basis. What do you appreciate about that person? Jot down your thoughts. Notice how your appreciation makes you feel. You can choose whether to share your appreciation directly with that person.

Write 5 things about yourself as a person for which you are grateful. If it's difficult to think of 5 things, focus on what other people have said they appreciate about you.

When I started
counting my
blessings, my whole
life turned around.

—

Wallace D. Wittles

What do you consider to be one of the greatest blessings in your life? Describe the blessing in detail using as many of your senses as possible. What does that blessing look like, what does it sound like, how does it make you feel?

Think about someone in your life who has recently shown you kindness in some way. Write a letter of gratitude to this person and deliver it to them personally.

Dear _____

YOUR NAME HERE

_____

_____

_____

_____

_____

_____

_____

Love,

_____

YOUR NAME HERE

Look inward and think about a personality trait or habit that you tend to think of as negative. Now look for a "silver lining," and write about how that trait has benefited you in some way, and how you are grateful for that trait. Maybe you tend to be a perfectionist, and that tendency helps you accomplish more of your goals. Or, perhaps you are exceedingly laid-back, which helps you let go of frustrations more easily.

The 5-Minute Happiness Journal

Reflect upon your present blessings, of which every man has plenty; not on your past misfortunes, of which all men have some.

Charles Dickens

Think about the past week and write about the events and circumstances that you are grateful for having happened. This can be especially helpful if you've had a difficult week. Focusing on the things for which you are grateful, rather than things that frustrate or annoy you, has the power to lead to lasting happiness.

Who is one person who had a positive influence on your life when you were young? What was it about that person or your relationship that made a difference in your life?

_____

_____

_____

_____

_____

_____

_____

_____

_____

_____

_____

_____

_____

_____

_____

_____

_____

An Affirmation
for Appreciation

*"I appreciate the many blessings in my life.
I choose to focus on all that is good and plentiful."*

Write this affirmation on an index card or sticky note
and keep it where you can see it on a regular basis.
Each time you read and repeat it, think about the
blessings in your life at that moment and express
appreciation for them.

Sit in the place in your home where you usually write in this journal. Look around you and write down what brings you happiness. A cozy chair, a beautiful work of art, a drawing from a child, the people or pets who live with you, etc. What do you notice in your home environment that makes you smile and feel content?

Savor the Outdoors

Take a 5-minute walk outside and focus on what you see, hear, feel, and smell. Look closely at the trees, flowers, or foliage. Listen for the sound of birds, or laughter, or the rustling of the wind. Take some deep breaths and notice what you smell. Take it all in and notice how you feel.

Cultivate the habit of being grateful for every good thing that comes to you, and to give thanks continuously. And because all things have contributed to your advancement, you should include all things in your gratitude.

———

Ralph Waldo Emerson

Write down 2 events in your life for which you are grateful: one that clearly brought something positive into your life and another that may be more difficult to see the benefit it brought.

Think about an event in your life for which you are grateful. It could even be the first event that you mentioned in the previous prompt. Spend 5 minutes thinking or writing about what your life would be like if that event had not occurred. This practice can help prevent you from taking positive events in your life for granted.

Think about something nice that a close friend or family member has done for you lately. Write about what happened in as much detail as you can remember. When you express gratitude to or about someone, your gratitude grows, especially when you are specific about what you appreciate about that person or what kindness that person has shown you.

A Gratitude Meditation

Sit in a comfortable position. Close your eyes and relax your shoulders. Take a few deep breaths. Place both hands over your heart, and feel a deep sense of gratitude for your heart, your physical body, and your health. Notice the breath as it moves in and out of your body, and express gratitude for the life force that is moving through you. Feel gratitude for the parts of you—such as your eyes that help you see, and your arms and legs that help you move about in the world. Notice your emotions, and feel a sense of gratitude for your ability to feel joy and connection to people and the world around you. Let this sense of gratitude grow as you take a few more deep breaths. Soften your focus and slowly open your eyes.

Think about a current circumstance in your life that feels stressful. Write down 5 things about the situation for which you can be grateful. You don't need to deny the stress or discomfort of the situation, but notice the little things that can help reduce the stress. For example, is there someone who has supported you in getting through the situation? Has the situation helped you become stronger in some way? Has it helped you have compassion and empathy for other people who may experience something similar?

I would maintain
that thanks are
the highest form
of thought;
and that gratitude
is happiness
doubled by wonder.

——

G. K. Chesterton

What arouses a sense of wonder or awe in you? This could be seeing the majesty of the mountains or hearing the unbridled laughter of a child. Allow that sense of awe to grow and fill you. Write down your thoughts and your feelings of gratitude and wonder.

A Simple Cup of Tea

As you make yourself a morning cup of tea or coffee, pause for a few minutes to give gratitude for this simple act of self-care. Listen to the sound of the boiling water, smell the aroma, feel the warmth in your hands, notice your senses awaken as you take the first sip. Be grateful for all that you have ahead of you on this day.

Think about a situation in your life that has felt like an obstacle or challenge. How can you gently shift your thinking and perspective to see that situation as a potential opportunity?

What is a belonging or possession that brings you happiness? It could be something big, like a car that helps you get where you need to go, or something small, like your favorite sweater. What about that belonging makes you happy and grateful?

_____

_____

_____

_____

_____

_____

_____

_____

_____

_____

_____

_____

_____

_____

Make a Gratitude List

Find a notebook or blank journal that you can designate as your gratitude journal. Set a schedule for yourself to write down 3 to 5 things that fill you with a sense of gratitude on a regular basis. Research tells us that it doesn't have to be done daily. Just keep your journal in a place where you will see it often. Take 5 minutes and write in your journal several times per week.

Write a few sentences about your current life circumstances. What have you overcome to be where you are today? What skills and talents have you developed that helped you in your journey?

_____

_____

_____

_____

_____

_____

_____

_____

_____

_____

_____

What are you looking forward to in the near future? What opportunities, dreams, and goals make you happy when you think about them? What do you hope to feel and accomplish in the next days, weeks, and months?

The mere
sense of
living is
joy enough.

—

Emily Dickinson

Write this quote by Emily Dickinson down on a sticky note or index card and place it where you will see it on a daily basis. Think about and use the space below to record 1 or 2 additional things in your life for which you are grateful.

Write down how you feel as you finish this journal. Write about the feelings of reflection, growth, acceptance, peace, happiness, gratitude, wonder, and joy that you have experienced. What has surprised you? What has changed since you started this process? Which practices did you find resonated most with you? Which practices would you like to continue?

Resources

Books

Ballard, Elise. *Epiphany: True Stories of Sudden Insight to Inspire, Encourage and Transform.* Temerity Publishing and Entertainment: 2014.

Clear, James. *Atomic Habits: An Easy & Proven Way to Build Good Habits & Break Bad Ones.* Avery: 2018.

Duhigg, Charles. The Power of Habit: Why We Do What We Do in Life and Business. New York: Random House, 2014.

Dweck, Carol S. *Mindset: The New Psychology of Success.* Random House, 2006.

Gilbert, Elizabeth. *Eat Pray Love: One Woman's Search for Everything Across Italy, India and Indonesia.* Riverhead Books, 2006.

Gwinn, J.D., Casey & Chan Hellman, Ph.D. *Hope Rising: How the Science of HOPE Can Change Your Life.* Morgan James Publishing, 2018.

Lyubomirsky, Sonja. *The How of Happiness: A New Approach to Getting the Life You Want.* Penguin Press, 2007.

Rubin, Gretchen. *The Happiness Project*. Harper Collins, 2009.

Organizations/Websites

Greater Good Science Center, University of California, Berkeley. An organization that offers many articles and resources related to happiness, including an online course called The Science of Happiness. The group's online magazine: www.greatergood.berkeley. edu.

Other helpful articles and further information:
www.mindsetworks.com
www.projecthappiness.org

References

Angelou, Maya. *Wouldn't Take Nothing for My Journey Now*. US: Random House, 1993. "I have found that among its other benefits, giving liberates the soul of the giver." Quoted on page 98.

Aristotle. *The Nicomachean Ethics* (Oxford World's Classics). New York: Oxford University Press, 2009. "Happiness depends upon ourselves." Quoted on page 2.

Ballard, Elise. *Epiphany: True Stories of Sudden Insight to Inspire, Encourage and Transform*. US: Harmony Books, 2014. Quoted on page 52.

Breines, Juliana. "Four Great Gratitude Strategies." *Greater Good Magazine*. Last modified June 30, 2015. https://www.greatergood.berkeley.edu/article/item/four_great_gratitude_strategies.

Chesterton, G. K. "I would maintain that thanks are the highest form of thought; and that gratitude is happiness doubled by wonder." Excerpt from an essay entitled "Christmas and Salesmanship", published December 1935. Quoted on page 124.

Collette, Amy. *The Gratitude Connection: Embrace the Positive Power of Thanks*. Louisville, CO: Wild Grace, 2015. "Gratitude is a powerful catalyst for happiness. It's the spark that lights a fire of joy in your soul." Quote on page 104.

Cummings, E.E. *E.E. Cummings: A Miscellany Revised*. US: October House, 1967. "The moment you feel, you're nobody-but-yourself—in a world which is doing its best, night and day, to make you everybody else—means to fight the hardest battle which any human being can fight. . . ." Quoted on page 56.

Dalai Lama. *The Art of Happiness*. New York: River-head Books, 2009. "Happiness is determined more by one's state of mind than by external events." Quoted on page 26.

Dickens, Charles. *A Christmas Carol and Other Stories*. US: Modern Library, 2001. "Reflect upon your present blessings-of which every man has many-not on your past misfortunes, of which all men have some." Quoted on page 112.

Dickinson, Emily. *Letters: Emily Dickinson*. US: Alfred A. Knopf, 2011. "Find ecstasy in life; the mere sense of living is joy enough." Quoted on page 132.

Disney, Walt. *Walt Disney: Conversations 2006*. Mississippi: University Press of Mississippi, 2006. "Happiness is a state of mind. It's just according to the way you look at things." Quoted on page 38.

Duhigg, Charles. *The Power of Habit: Why We Do What We Do in Life and Business*. New York: Random House, 2014.

Dweck, Carol S. *Mindset: The New Psychology of Success*. New York: Random House, 2006.

Gilbert, Elizabeth. *Eat Pray Love: One Woman's Search for Everything Across Italy, India and Indonesia*. New York: Riverhead Books, 2006. "Happiness is the consequence of personal effort. You fight for it, strive for it, insist upon it, and sometimes even travel around the world looking for it … And once you have achieved a state of happiness, you must never become lax about maintaining it. You must make a mighty effort to keep swimming upward into that happiness forever, to stay afloat on top of it." Quoted on page 42.

Gotter, Ana. "Understanding Emotional Numbness." *Healthline*. Last modified May 23, 2017. https://www.healthline.com/health/feeling-numb.

Hanh, Thich Nhat. *No Mud, No Lotus: The Art of Transforming Suffering*. Berkeley: Parallax Press, 2014. "So many conditions of happiness are available—more than enough for you to be happy right now. You don't have to run into the future in order to get more." Quoted on page vii.

Harvard Health Publishing. "Giving Thanks Can Make You Happier." Accessed November 3, 2018. https://www.health.harvard.edu/healthbeat /giving-thanks-can-make-you-happier.

Hopper, Elizabeth. "Can Helping Others Help You Find Meaning in Life?" *Greater Good Magazine*. Last

modified February 16, 2016. https://www.greatergood
.berkeley.edu/article/item/can_helping_others_help
_you_find_meaning_in_life.

Hopper, Elizabeth. "Four Ways Gratitude Helps You
with Difficult Feelings." Greater Good Magazine. Last
modified November 25, 2019. https://greatergood.
berkeley.edu/article/item/four_ways_gratitude_helps_
you_with_difficult_feelings.

Hopper, Elizabeth. "To Be Happier, Should You Focus
on Yourself or Others?" *Greater Good Magazine*. Last
modified September 9, 2019. http://www.greatergood.
berkeley.edu/article/item/to_be_happier_should_you_
focus_on_yourself_or_others.

James, Geoffrey. "Neuroscience Says Your Body and
Mind Get Stronger When You Focus on This One
Thing." *Inc.* July 5, 2019. https://www.inc.com
/geoffrey-james/neuroscience-says-your-body-mind-
get-stronger-when-you-focus-on-this-one-
thingdraft-1562273865.html.

James, William. *The Principles of Psychology*. US:
Dover Publications, 1950. "Action may not always
bring happiness, but there is no happiness without
action." Quoted on page 84.

Jobs, Steve. *BusinessWeek*. May 25, 1998. "Simple
can be harder than complex: You have to work hard
to get your thinking clean to make it simple." Quoted
on page 18.

Kanigel, Rachele. "How Laughter Yoga Heals, Plus 6 Fun Exercises to Try." *Yoga Journal*. Last modified September 5, 2018. https://www.yogajournal.com /lifestyle/laughter-cure.

Keller, Helen. *The Open Door* (quote page 11). US: Doubleday & Company, 1957. "When one door of happiness closes, another opens; but often we look so long at the closed door that we do not see the one which has been opened for us." Quoted on page 22.

Linde, Sharon. "Reticular Activating System: Defini-tion & Function." Accessed August 20, 2019. https://www.study.com/academy/lesson/reticular -activating-system-definition-function.html.

Lyubomirsky, Sonja. *The How of Happiness: A New Approach to Getting the Life You Want*. New York: Penguin, 2008.

Maraboli, Steve. *Unapologetically You: Reflections on Life and the Human Experience*. US: A Better Today Publishing: 2013. "Happiness is a state of mind, a choice, a way of living; it is not something to be achieved, it is something to be experienced." Quoted on page 10.

Melville, Henry. "Partaking in Other Men's Sins" (sermon), from January 2 to December 18, 1855, in "The Golden Lectures," transcript, https://melvilliana. blogspot.com/2013/02/henry-melvills-thousand-fi-bres-and.html. "Ye live not for yourselves; ye cannot live for yourselves ; a thousand fibres connect you with your fellow-men, and along those fibres, as along sympathetic threads, run your actions as causes, and return to you as effects." Quoted on page 72.

Merton, Thomas. *No Man is an Island*. US: Mariner Books, 2002. "We cannot be happy if we expect to live all the time at the highest peak of intensity. Happiness is not a matter of intensity but of balance and order and rhythm and harmony." Quoted on page 16.

Mikulak, Anna. "All About Awe." Association for Psychological Science. Last modified April 2015. https://www.psychologicalscience.org/observer /all-about-awe.

Morin, Amy. *7 Scientifically Proven Benefits of Gratitude That Will Motivate You to Give Thanks Year-Round*. Forbes. Last modified November 23, 2014. https://www.forbes.com/sites/amymorin /2014/11/23/7-scientifically-proven-benefits-of -gratitude-that-will-motivate-you-to-give -thanks-year-round/#3337ec99183c.

Nelson, Willie. *The Tao of Willie: A Guide to the Happiness in Your Heart*. US: Avery, 2007. "When I started counting my blessings, my whole life turned around." Quoted on page 108.

Newman, Kira M. "Three Emerging Insights About Happiness." *Greater Good Magazine*. Last modified August 5, 2019.

https://www.greatergood.berkeley.edu/article/item/three_emerging_insights_about_happiness.

Rogers, Fred. *You are Special: Neighborly Wit and Wisdom from Mr. Rogers*. China: Running Press, 2002. "As human beings, our job in life is to help people realize how rare and valuable each one of us really is, that each of us has something that no one else has- or ever will have- something inside that is unique to all time. It's our job to encourage each other to discover that uniqueness and to provide ways of developing its expression." Quoted on page 66.

Roosevelt, Franklin D. "First Inaugural Address," March 4, 1933, United States Capitol, Washington, D.C., transcript https://millercenter.org/the-presidency/presidential-speeches/march-4-1933-first-inaugural-address. "Happiness lies in the joy of achievement and the thrill of creative effort." Quoted on page 92.

Rubin, Gretchen. *The Happiness Project*. New York: Harper Collins, 2009.

Rumi, Jalal al-Din. *The Essential Rumi, New Expanded Edition*. US: HarperOne: May 28, 2004. "You are not just a drop in the ocean, you are the mighty ocean in the drop." Quote on page 100.

Smith, Jeremy Adam. "Six Habits of Highly Grateful People." *Greater Good Magazine*. November 20, 2013. https://www.greatergood.berkeley.edu/article/item/six_habits_of_highly_grateful_people.

Stanborough, Rebecca Joy. "Smiling with Your Eyes: What Exactly Is a Duchenne Smile?" *Healthline.* Last modified June 29, 2019. https://www.healthline.com/health/duchenne-smile.

Wattles, Wallace D. *The Science of Getting Rich.* US: CreateSpace Independent Publishing Platform, 2015. "Cultivate the habit of being grateful for every good thing that comes to you, and to give thanks continuously. And because all things have contributed to your advancement, you should include all things in your gratitude." Quoted on page 118.

Wong, Joel, and Joshua Brown. "How Gratitude Changes You and Your Brain." *Greater Good Magazine.* Last modified June 6, 2017. https://www.greatergood.berkeley.edu/article/item/how_gratitude_changes_you_and_your_brain.

Acknowledgments

As I was making some major changes in my life ten years ago, I read Elizabeth Gilbert's book *Eat Pray Love*. I posted this quote on Facebook as a reminder to myself to continue to fight for my happiness:

"And when you sense a faint potentiality for happiness after such dark times you must grab onto the ankles of that happiness and not let go until it drags you face-first out of the dirt—this is not selfishness, but obligation. You were given life; it is your duty to find something beautiful within life no matter how slight."

Ten years later, that quote popped up in my "memories" on Facebook—the very same week that I was asked to write this book. Writing this book has given me an opportunity to reflect on how much my life has changed since the original post. I met and married the man of my dreams and doubled the size of my family. Our kids are growing up and becoming compassionate, talented, and happy young adults. I've continued to thrive in a career that I love. My husband and I have built two businesses, and we have moved to the place where we want to spend the rest of our lives. I live a life of true happiness and have become a better version of myself because of the love that I share with my family: my husband, Michael, and our kids—Marisa, Christian, Thomas, and Olivia.

Yes, life continues with its ups and downs, happiness and sadness, comedy and tragedy. Even during the writing of this book, life threw a few curveballs, and I wondered if I would be able to complete the book according to my commitment. My greatest teachers have always been the clients that I work with as a social worker. From my early days working in homeless shelters to my current work with seniors who have seen all aspects of life, my clients have taught me that happiness can be found anywhere, any time. While experiencing poverty, trauma, and terminal illness, they have taught me that I can always find something for which I am grateful. They have taught me this by their example, by living in a state of happiness and gratitude no matter their current life circumstances. This book exists because of what they have taught me.

The reflections and practices in this book are exactly what I practice to keep myself in a state of happiness, gratitude, joy, and willingness to embrace all that life has to offer, even in the messy middle of life. It is my greatest hope that this book has helped you connect to a deeper sense of happiness and continue to press onward to make all of your hopes and dreams come true.

Thank you to Vanessa Putt and the team at Callisto Media who have given me another opportunity to write a book on a topic that is near and dear to my heart. A special word of gratitude to Emily Angell for her kindness, patience, understanding, and encouragement through the process.

About the Author

 Leslie Marchand is a licensed clinical social worker, founder of SoYoCo Wellness, TEDx speaker, and author of *The Self-Love Journal: Banish Self-Doubt and Learn to Love Yourself.* She writes and teaches about personal wellness, professional self-care, and how to renew yourself and inspire others through her blog and online courses at www.SoYoCo.org

In addition to her 25-year career as a clinical social worker, Leslie is a registered yoga teacher and certified life coach and spends her free time reading the latest research, books, and articles on wellness, positive psychology, personal development, and entrepreneurship. She and her husband live on their organic and pasture-based farm in Texas with their four kids, eight dogs, dozens of pigs, hundreds of turkeys, thousands of chickens, and acres of produce.

CPSIA information can be obtained
at www.ICGtesting.com
Printed in the USA
LVHW011002290320
651528LV00001B/1